Nonprofit Success Strategies: Volume 1

Putting the Profit in Nonprofit

5 Power Success Strategies for Nonprofits

By Mari-Anne Kehler and Andrew Bird

"Consciously or unconsciously, every one of us does render some service or other. If we cultivate the habit of doing this service deliberately, our desire for service will steadily grow stronger, and will make, not only for our own happiness, but that of the world at large." ~ Mohandas Gandhi

ISBN: 1500699616
ISBN 13: 9781500699611
Library of Congress Control Number: 2014913798
CreateSpace Independent Publishing Platform
North Charleston, South Carolina

What the nonprofit community is saying

I worked under Mari-Anne and Andrew for four years at Deloitte, where they mentored and supported me to develop a nonprofit outside of work. I modeled our organization's culture after their results-oriented leadership styles and that is what empowered our decentralized movement to go from a small group of students partnering with a handful of Honduran communities to a global international nonprofit with $15 million in annual revenue that now sends more annual volunteers than the Peace Corps.
— *Steven Atamian*
Co-Founder, Global Brigades

When our organization was looking to grow and gain eminence, Mari-Anne launched the FRED Conference for Golden Heart Ranch as a vehicle to raise our national profile. She has done that and far more. FRED is the premier organization promoting adult special needs housing, employment and quality of life. Mari-Anne is renowned for her ability to originate creative ideas, then exceed all expectations with their outcomes.
— *Rose Hein*
Golden Heart Ranch, Founder

This book is… "an invaluable tool for any growing nonprofit and it's full of clear ideas to start the process of professionalizing key nonprofit duties like fundraising and volunteer recruitment."
— *Elaine Hall*
Founder, Project Miracle

Having had a career at Dell, Inc. then co-founding a nonprofit, it's critical to use business as the model to succeed and make an impact. With their experience and clear definition of the 5 Power Success Strategies, Mari-Anne Kehler and Andrew

Bird have taken the best practices of business and applied them to running a successful nonprofit. Faster, better, smarter... any growing nonprofit will achieve these results by following the material in this book!
— Ann Duncan Levy
Impact Giving, Co-Founder

Andrew's deep knowledge of volunteer strategy, fundraising and nonprofit management was an important part of the tremendous success of the University of Santa Monica's SpiritWalk. With his help, we built an integrated support structure and raised more than $100,000 in our first annual event — more than doubling our fundraising goal. Andrew's professionalism, knowledge, creativity, passion, enthusiasm and commitment were inspiring. With his help, we were able to co-create and manifest an event that far surpassed our highest vision for what could be possible!
— Amy Knedlik, M.A.
Co-founder and Operations Leader, University of Santa Monica SpiritWalk event

Foreword

When you start a nonprofit because of a pressing need in your life and the community, there isn't a roadmap. There's just an intense desire to do **something** to help, to change what isn't working and make a difference.

That's how I started The Miracle Project over 10 years ago. I'm an acting coach by trade and my life changed the day I adopted my son from Russia, who soon after was diagnosed with autism. When traditional therapies weren't helping him, I sought guidance from more progressive experts in the field of autism who encouraged me to use my acting background and creativity to reach my son. For example, if he spun in circles, I would spin with him and turn it into a game of 'ring-around-the rosies.' When I followed his lead, we'd connect and laugh together. Seeing this success, I brought other theater friends in to help me. I taught my colleagues everything I was learning about autism, trading audition coaching in exchange for them creatively bridging a connection with my son's world — 10 hours a day, 7 days a week. Slowly, my son emerged into our world. However, the strain of my involvement with my son was so intense that my marriage broke up and I found myself alone and broke with a child in need and few options. A friend suggested I develop a group theater program for other children with disabilities. I wrote a grant proposal in two days and was miraculously awarded $40,000 — I truly believe angels supported me, and that support has continued.

Our first season of The Miracle Project was extraordinary. Children with autism and other disabilities performed an original musical alongside peers without disabilities — connecting, making friends and doing what some "experts" deemed impossible. Filmmakers heard of my work, documented a season, and this turned into *Autism: The Musical,* an Emmy award-winning film that has had frequent HBO and OWN showings.

It wasn't as easy it sounds — having no experience in nonprofit management or business of any sort, I didn't know how to sustain the organization each year. But I saw what a difference The Miracle Project was making in so many people's lives and I didn't want to stop. I supported my program, myself and my son by working around the clock, coaching professional actors in my home and on TV and film sets — I was exhausted and almost gave up. But then I was asked to merge my nonprofit into a much larger one. However, when *Autism: The Musical* came out and then screened at the United Nations, I received thousands of requests to replicate my program around the world. I felt the pressing need to answer these requests, but this was not the mission of the larger nonprofit. I had to separate and begin anew but I did not have the funds or bodies or hours to make that happen. The need was there. We just had to find a way to meet that need. I had to establish a new nonprofit and start the climb up another mountain.

Under our new name, Project Miracle, we have a big vision to go global and provide well-funded programs in every community that needs them. This is my life's work, and the angels keep coming to help make it happen. I've discovered that to grow from a founder-driven organization to a global nonprofit will take resources and abilities far beyond what I alone can bring to the table. It takes professional, business-driven skills, strategies and tactics to get where I want to go. That's where *Putting the Profit in Nonprofit: 5 Power Success Strategies for Nonprofits* comes in. It's an invaluable tool for any growing nonprofit and it's full of clear ideas to start the process of professionalizing key nonprofit duties like fundraising and volunteer recruitment. The authors are among the many angels that have helped me along the way — I believe there is a profound need in the nonprofit community for this book's insights.

At Project Miracle we're busily fundraising so we can hire additional staff to keep growing. I'm focused on our big picture goals and I'm excited to continue to evolve, just like so many nonprofit founders out there.

I wish all of you luck on your path and I hope you'll use the strategies in this book, as I have, as one of your ways to achieve long-term success. Most importantly, never give up.

Elaine Hall ("Coach E!"), Project Miracle
Founder, The Miracle Project (www.themiracleproject.org)
Author: *Now I See the Moon* (HarperCollins 2010) and *Seven Keys to Unlock Autism* (Wiley 2011)
One of the stars of *Autism: The Musical*

Table of Contents

Introduction

Is your nonprofit raising enough money?

The National Center for Charitable Statistics (NCCS) maintains a database on U.S. nonprofits and charitable activities. According to the NCCS, there are currently over 1.5 million nonprofit organizations in the United States. This is a magnificent thing, since it means many, many people are seeking to help others. It's not so magnificent to think that many organizations with great intentions are asking for the same scarce donations and resources you are, especially when economics are more volatile.

People who are involved in the nonprofit world as staff, volunteers, board members or donors have nagging questions… *"Are we reaching enough potential donors? How do we convince people to volunteer their time? Where do we find people willing to give? How do we get those people to actually write a check? Is there more we could do to raise the money we need to fulfill our mission? How do we juggle the demands of running an organization with the demands of fundraising?"*

Ripped from the pages of big business best practices, the Success Strategies give your nonprofit the opportunity to do it faster, better and smarter.

By definition, many nonprofits were founded by people profoundly affected by a particular need or desire — perhaps they helped someone through an illness, had a disabled child, want music back in the schools, or they are motivated by any of a host of other things. So they went out and took action to help their cause. Bravo!

But nonprofits are businesses, and managing a nonprofit means running a business. Founders may not have a background in nonprofit management, and may not be sure what to do next in getting their organization off the ground or going to the next level. They may feel discouraged by the economy, by volunteers drifting away, or they have struggled just to keep their heads above water in administrative survival mode. Added to these challenges is the fact that the world has been changing at lightning speed and there are new modes of communication emerging all the time.

By following the 5 Power Success Strategies we discuss in this book, any nonprofit can think like a business CEO and forge a new fundraising path, find great volunteers, develop stronger relationships with donors, define a clear message and raise more money in less time.

The authors of this book have served as marketing leaders at multi-billion dollar companies and have served on numerous nonprofit boards. Just like most volunteers, we were drawn to serve nonprofits based on our own interests — for Mari-Anne, it was helping her son face the challenges of autism; for Andrew it was a passion for the arts and mentoring young people. Mari-Anne and Andrew have a long history of bringing their business insights and skills to their nonprofit work, and now you can benefit from their experience too.

Ripped from the pages of big business best practices, the Success Strategies give your nonprofit the opportunity to do it faster, better and smarter. Oh yeah, and you'll raise more money!

Due to the times we cyclically live in, donations can be harder to come by for many nonprofits. When there are dips in economic stability, we don't recommend waiting for happier times. It will take less than two hours to read this book, so read on and start using these 5 Power Success Strategies today.

Why you should listen to big business strategies

Kill or be killed.

According to the Internal Revenue Service (IRS) Data Book for 2012, there were 1,484,818 501(c) organizations for the fiscal year ending in September 2012. That year the IRS approved 52,615 organizations for tax-exempt status, out of 60,793 applications — an approval rate of 86.5 percent. That's 144 new nonprofits being born every day, and all of them are competing for donations, volunteers and other much-needed resources.

Big business has spent the time and money to find the best ways to make the biggest possible profit. Nonprofits don't have those kinds of resources — and even if they did, they perhaps wouldn't prioritize spending them on leading edge business strategy. Why not just steal from the best and adapt it to your own needs? In business, we call it "leveraging" and not stealing, by the way.

This isn't a book about the perfect silent auction, selling candy, affinity programs, car washes, or planning an amazing "thon" (as in walk-a, bike-a, dance-a, or bake-a). There are plenty of sources for that, and we're not advising against them — in fact, there is a nice chunk of money to be made from these tactics.

> *Why not just steal from the best*
> *and adapt it to your own needs?*

Tactics like events, thons, products and sponsorships are useful and effective. We love tactics. But often these tactics stand alone, and may not be connected to the bigger picture, which is always about having the resources to serve the cause of the nonprofit, its staff, board and volunteers.

Although this was written by two corporate veterans, it's not even a book about the much-discussed "next big things" like corporate volunteerism or corporate matching donations.

So what IS this all about? In a word, RESULTS. Results come from a clear strategy designed to find the best ways to use your limited resources to reap the maximum benefits. In this book we've outlined 5 Power Success Strategies that will drive results. We'll give you some practical tools to use in your quest to:

1. Define and communicate your organization's core message

2. Recruit an army of committed volunteers

3. Target the donors that are most likely to open their wallets

4. Create the donor relationships that will pay off

5. Keep your eye on the big picture, so you can focus on the right activities

So let's move right into the Power Success Strategies. It all begins with defining your organization in a way that is clear and easily communicated.

Chapter 1: the first Power Success Strategy — define yourself (then tell everyone)

People can't give you money if they don't understand who you are and who you help. They also can't give you money if YOU can't effectively explain who you are and who you help!

Why does your organization exist? Whom do you serve? In big business, we call this a mission. No matter what you call it, can every volunteer, staff member and board member sum up the mission in a sentence or two? If they can't, you've just identified your #1 barrier to success.

Andrew's story

Everyone I meet hears the description of Global Brigades, an organization where I'm on the board: *"Global Brigades sends over 10,000 college student service volunteers every year to Central America and Africa to do health, water, architecture and business brigades that empower people to improve their lives."* Once they hear this from me, they inevitably ask questions and want to know how to help. (By the way, if you want to know more, go to www.brigades.org).

Mari-Anne's story

Golden Heart Ranch has a clear mission: "we are dedicated to building a living community where adults with special needs can safely live, learn and work side by side with their community." Until we were able to clearly articulate our mission, all the good intentions in the world couldn't further our fundraising efforts! (For more information, go to www.goldenheartranch.org).

Focus on your key message

In business, a clear message is the building block of strategic planning. Strategy is what then allows each unique brand to develop. The brand's strength and clarity translate to more sales, and profits are the goal. The team comes together to chart the best course to reach the goal. Everyone there is getting paid, and getting paid depends on making a profit. It's simplistic, but no smart businesses try to be all things to all people.

But let's take a look at nonprofits. Nonprofits tend to have a mix of people involved who may have their own ideas and needs that translate into different priorities. Only a few may be getting paid, and even they are not solely motivated by the money. The mission can expand to satisfy too many needs and too many people — it can get muddy, and the primary goals start to get lost in translation. Business guru Stephen Covey once said "the main thing is to keep the main thing the main thing." When businesses discover they have ventured too far from their core goals, they realize they need to re-group and re-focus. A great example of this is Apple after Steve Jobs left — management decided to widely diversify and the stock price crashed. When Jobs returned, he immediately cut the product line to the core. Another example is when Starbucks decided to offer grilled sandwiches — when customers smelled the heavy cooking aromas, they complained. They wanted Starbucks to smell like coffee and Starbucks quickly made the change. They went back to basics and profits boomed, once again.

So getting known is essentially about focus. How can you develop a strong, core message that can be repeated by everyone associated with your organization? How do you make sure your message has heart, meaning and is compelling?

There are three clear areas we suggest you focus on — what, how, who:

1. Message — **what** your organization does to help others

2. Goal(s) — **how** you'll focus

3. Communicating the message and goal(s) — **who** you'll tell

A clear, impactful message helps your organization in everything you do — attracting volunteers, motivating staff, recruiting board members, and of course in fundraising.

Recurring Theme #1: the 80/20 Rule

Throughout this book, we often refer to something called the 80/20 Rule. Also known as the Pareto Principle, the 80/20 Rule states that, for many events, roughly 80% of the effects come from 20% of the causes. In big business, it's used as a rule of thumb to help us focus, with the knowledge that using 20% of the most efficient resources will create 80% of the profit.

In the nonprofit world, we want to find a way to identify and focus on the 20% of the donors that will produce 80% of the donations. We also want to put this type of focused effort into finding the best volunteers, corporate donors/sponsors, marketing materials, etc. — in other words, we want to concentrate on using the least amount of resources to get the maximum results in any given situation. In business, it's called efficiency!

There are an almost unlimited number of ways to apply the 80/20 Rule. Keep it in mind as you read on.

The message

You're at a cocktail party (or lunch with a new friend, or watching your kids play soccer, or in a job interview) and someone asks you, *"So, what do you do?"* You might recite your job title, mention your kids, say that you're in school, or describe a hobby or leisure passion.

When you tell someone you are involved with a nonprofit, they inevitably ask *"so what do THEY do?"* It sounds like an easy question, but people are likely to launch into an explanation of why they're involved (*"my child has autism and I got involved to give back"*, or *"I love going to the theater and I love being around theater people"*, or even *"I'm trying to get into college and I need experience for my application."*) Yeah, but what does the nonprofit DO?

By defining a shared purpose and a common message, you are creating instant word of mouth and planting your organization's message and goals into peoples' heads. The simpler the better. In business, we call it an elevator pitch — if you're riding in an elevator with someone, how would you describe your business quickly, before the elevator doors open? Businesspeople also call it a Value Proposition; for nonprofits, it's commonly called a Mission Statement. Let's take it a step further and call it an Impact Statement.

> *By defining a shared purpose and a common message,*
> *you are creating instant word of mouth and planting your*
> *organization's message and goals into peoples' heads.*

Brainstorm your Impact Statement

Gather as many of your organizations' stakeholders in one room as you can — staff, volunteers, board members, even the people who are receiving help from your organization's mission. It could be a virtual room if you're all spread out, but in person is best so that ideas can flow and feed off of one another.

There are no right or wrong answers in a brainstorming session — write it all down and sort it out as a next step. Ask for statements that reflect the effect or impact of the organization's services and describe how the community's needs are being met. Answer key questions with your statements:

- Why was our organization founded?

- What do we do better than anyone else?

- What is (or will be) our biggest achievement?

- How will peoples' lives be better after we provide our service(s)?

- What emotions will people feel after they've been helped by us?

It is extremely tempting to focus on how great your organization is and list all that you've accomplished. Don't do it. In the marketing world, what sways customers is the clear impact you have and the transformation you can expect by using these services. Here is an example from a fictional nonprofit:

- **Current mission:** "Because our neighborhood isn't always safe and we were worried about our kids after school, we founded Nonprofit XYZ to keep them busy until we got off work. Former schoolteachers who really care offer homework help and there are also safe and fun physical activities like volleyball, jump rope, and hopscotch, as well as crafts like finger painting, knitting, jewelry-making, etc. Also, we've won awards from the city and other organizations because we really care about kids."

- **Impact-focused mission example:** "Nonprofit XYZ offers specialized after-school programs taught by experienced teachers to enrich at-risk youth."

The old mission is scattered and unfocused and probably won't make anyone pick up the telephone to enroll. The impact-focused mission goes right to the impact the organization will have on you and your child. I'd call them right now before they're full for the semester (if they existed, that is!)

In the end, you'll have an easier path to finding the core mission, one that can be repeated by everyone in the organization. We're all leading busy lives and can be easily distracted by multiple messages at any given time — so we suggest you find ways to repeat the mission as part of every communication, far beyond the point of redundancy, to allow your audiences to "get it".

Bonuses of a focused message

A focused message also has some surprising and important by-products that can benefit your cause:

- First and foremost is the concept of buy-in — those participating in developing the message exercise will feel like an owner of the message, and will be more likely to feel even more committed to its success.

- Second, by keeping it simple and clear, your message can more easily be spread person-to-person — everyone becomes your ambassador!

- Third, your compelling message gets people excited about the RESULTS of what you achieve!

TIP: Another interesting by-product can be found in the world of social media — by repeating certain keywords wherever you can, you are literally raising the status of your organization in Google searches. For those of you who are (or want to be) savvy in the social media world, search for the AdWords tool on Google and do some research.

Focus on your core goal

Your nonprofit's goals can be as varied as its team, but this is the time to get serious about choosing one. That's right, ONE. If you're struggling to pick just one, know that pouring your energy into a core goal will make it possible to expand later, with lots of lessons learned. In fact, it's the only way you'll grow successfully.

Your one goal can have lots of activities associated with it, but don't confuse those with goals. Goals should be measured by the impact they have on your constituents rather than a dollar amount or press mentions — what exactly is the change your organization is trying to accomplish and what defines that change?

Don't forget — be focused. Specific, measurable, attainable, relevant, timely sales goals work. Muddy goals that cobble together many personal goals of your team don't work. See Chapter 6 for more on goals.

Now tell everyone

You know who you are. You have a focused goal. Now you have a story to tell that will define you in the market — this is your branding. Brands are simple stories that carry through everything you say about your organization.

Put your message on your homepage. Put it on your business cards. Write articles about it for the local press. Make a big banner that says it and put it up at every event. Put it on your outgoing telephone message. Put it permanently at the bottom of every email. Put it to music. Whatever it takes. Repeat, repeat, repeat!

3 key takeaways:

1. The most important message is about how the customer will be impacted by your service

2. Great Impact Statements are about focusing on a simple message that can be easily communicated and repeated

3. The Impact Statement is the core building block for your brand

"If you can't explain it simply, you don't understand it well enough."
~Albert Einstein

Chapter 2: the second Power Success Strategy — how to recruit an army of volunteers

"We have a small core of dedicated volunteers".

"We don't know what we'd ever do without Jim — he's a dynamo!"

"My goodness, Marge has run this event for years — I wouldn't know the first thing about how to do it if she ever left."

Uh-oh, we've heard that before. Raise your hands if your organization's work is carried out by a small number of "dedicated" people. That's what we thought. We love them — they're the people whose hands shoot up when a project arises. Unfortunately, they're the same people that can ultimately burn out and leave or forget to empower others to share project responsibilities.

But what if there were dozens, even hundreds of people who could step forward, joyfully giving and getting their needs met in return? There are!

Once again, this is about focusing, so let's break out some core volunteer sources:

- Low-hanging fruit

- Likely sympathizers

- Referrals

- People with specific skills

Low-hanging fruit: expand your reach

Have you taken a systematic look at who is most likely to be a supporter of your organization? In business, we have a phrase we like to use to describe missing the obvious: "Ignore the low-hanging fruit at your own peril." Many of us are so concerned with strategizing how to meet new people (the fruit higher up on the tree), that we may overlook the juicy ripe pool of volunteers who are open and receptive to being picked. No ladder required. Oh yeah, but you gotta ask 'em! We'll get to that in a minute.

Make a list of everyone that has been DIRECTLY touched by your organization. We say "directly" because the case has already been made to these people. Obvious areas might be:

- Current volunteers

- Past volunteers

- People who are or have been served by your organization

- Parents and family members of people who are or have been served by your organization

- Attendees of any event you have held in the past five years

- Vendors (whoever sells you the stuff you need to run your organization or your events)

Ignore the low-hanging fruit at your own peril.

If you don't have a mailing list, this is the time to create one. Be sure you are managing the list and capture anything that may be helpful about their connection (what event they attended, who they know, how much time or money they donated, what merchandise they donated and why/when, etc.)

We didn't want to mention the word "spreadsheet", but that's what this actually is — and yes, someone must be designated to manage and update the spreadsheet. A volunteer, perhaps! In business, we have many customer relationship management tools that can cost a little or a lot, but it all starts with a spreadsheet.

Low-hanging fruit is a numbers game. Don't spend time on hard-to-woo volunteers. This is about quickly and efficiently reaching out to the people who already believe. Look for organizations that are dependent on large numbers of volunteers and see what they're doing — Habitat for Humanity, large churches or even political campaigns are good examples.

A quick way to identify low-hanging fruit

Have all your key players make a list of exactly 10 possible new volunteers. Rank each 1-10 by their likelihood to say "yes" to an invitation to help your organization. Then ask the top five. Keep the bottom five aside — we'll get to them in a minute.

Likely sympathizers

We're still talking about focusing, and likely sympathizers are people who know you or your organization but need more attention and information to actually become a part of your team. These people can be grouped and approached that way. In business, we think of these groupings as portfolios rather than individual stocks — the groups share certain key characteristics and a common approach can be taken to the group and its members.

What are the groupings for your nonprofit? It can be as simple as "friends of Mari-Anne", whose common bond is the fact that they know her, respect her and love her and would be receptive to an invitation from her to learn more about the organization. Perhaps it's a group of professional women. Or it's tennis-lovers. Or lawyers. Or theater-goers. You can see where this is going — there are unlimited possibilities.

Then craft a tailored message that meets their need or interest. Again, the possibilities are endless — you could put together a mini-event (a lunch, tennis game, etc.) with like-minded people and add structure to the discussion where they can see themselves as a team and how they could fit into your organization.

Find a current volunteer or staff member who shares their interest and empower them to lead the group — this is win-win, as everyone will at least make contacts or relationships in areas where they have interest, whether they choose to volunteer for you or not. Keep the meetings focused on a specific outcome or outcomes and remember to empower the group (along with the leader) to accomplish a goal.

It should take 1-3 meetings with groups of likely sympathizers to get them started as volunteers. If they don't quickly see the value in giving some of their time, then move them off the list and into the longer-term prospect category.

> *But what if there were dozens, even hundreds of people who could step forward, joyfully giving and getting their needs met in return? There are!*

Referrals

It might seem obvious, but we can't say it enough: REFERRALS ARE GOLD. It might not seem obvious to some people, so ASK them to bring additional volunteers. Think of it this way: if someone you like and trust recommends something, you are much more likely to consider it for yourself. This applies to everything from good novels to dentists, so why shouldn't it apply to where you volunteer?

We covered this a bit in the low-hanging fruit section, but this is where you take it out to a wider audience, perhaps those five people you lopped off your Top 10 list. You ranked them lower for a reason, and this is the place where you can take a more marketing-oriented approach. Remember the key message about your organization — this is where it can be repeated loud and often.

You can also tailor a specific message that speaks directly to your referrals — perhaps they have a family member who could be helped by your organization, or they are politically interested in a certain topic, or your nonprofit is riding a wave of public enthusiasm and they could be part of a winning movement. Make it cool to be a part of your team! There are many, many possibilities.

Asking for referrals

Taking action is an important part of the referral process. Ask your "true believers" and staff to give you the names of three potential volunteers. You can then decide whether to take a personal approach or group them and tackle it that way. By breaking it down into these smaller chunks, dozens of potential volunteers can stack up quickly.

Volunteers with specific skills

Not everyone is a "worker bee" type of volunteer — they might have specific skills that can make your life easier, or they may be able to provide services that you would otherwise need to pay big bucks for. From accountants to lawyers to plumbers, it's important to understand who your potential volunteers are and how they can be used in the best possible way.

Remember how we mentioned portfolios?
Here's where you diversify!

This is especially true of board development, where you want to build a mix of experiences and skills for success. Board development is outside the scope of this book — we'll go through some more tools for building relationships in the next Power Success Strategy, so don't be dismayed if you don't have a ready pool of lawyers waiting to step up and work for free.

You may also have people who believe in your mission but are more interested in leading a specific project or business unit. Great! Ask them to recruit their team and empower them to deliver a specific result. They may have a team already in place they can bring (a family or a department at their workplace) or they may have wonderful contacts with specific skills.

The bottom line is to know your volunteers and how they are aligned with your mission. Honor their skills, strengths and desires for the type of contribution they can make, and go for it.

Recurring Theme #2: What's in it for me? (WIIFM)

Everyone's busy. Even if they like you or your cause, why exactly should a volunteer consider giving their time and/or money? Don't assume just giving back is a selling point — that can be applied to any nonprofit. Why YOUR organization? Finding what's in it for them provides them with powerful motivation to enthusiastically support you. Here are some possibilities to get you started, but remember that each person has unique needs and often they have more than one:

- I have a passion I've never been able to apply to my work life

- I need to learn a new, specific skill to be considered for the next job in my career

- I want to meet other people who share my concern about an issue

- I want to be part of a movement to really make the world a better place

- I want to use my skills beyond my workplace

- I'm retired and I want to be active and engaged

- I am applying for college and it's very competitive. I need to show I care about a cause

- I want to build relationships with your board members that could help me in my business

- I'm new in town and I want to get to know people

- I want to be of service and give back

- We're a big corporation and we want to be seen as community-friendly

- We're a big corporation and we want to do something that differentiates us from our competition

Finding the right message to motivate your volunteers is important, but following up and actually meeting their need is even more critical. Make sure they get what they came for and you will have a dedicated and satisfied volunteer. How do you find out? Ask them!

Answer objections

It's easy to shoot down a request that includes more work for us. *"It's a great cause, but I'm really busy with my family right now." "I'm starting a business and it's taking a lot of my time." "I'm looking to get promoted and am working extra hours."* Whatever the objection is, you have an opportunity to answer it before it becomes a no. When building relationships with your volunteers, jump in early with your answers to anticipated questions and throw in some WIIFM to seal the deal.

Brainstorm all possible objections with your team ahead of time and develop great messages (*"you probably thought this would take a lot of time, but the committee meetings are just two hours a month and I've seen people network really effectively and get new business!"*) The process doesn't end there — as you take the time to get to know your volunteers (and you WILL), keep looking for possible objections that might crop up in the future. People usually telegraph them if you haven't anticipated everything, so keep your ears and eyes open for clues. And, don't forget to keep reminding them of what's in it for them!

Lead your volunteers

This isn't a book about leadership, but there are a few key things we do in big business that can make a big impact on keeping your volunteers happy and contributing. Some are obvious, some may not be:

- **Smart delegating** — your volunteers aren't there to just do grunt work. Give them meaningful jobs and explain the need for their work, and they'll jump to do the grunt work that comes with it. If you just stop by their desk and throw some envelopes and labels at them, they might not be as enthusiastic. Remember to leverage their special skills or those they want to develop.

- **Spread the wealth** — it may seem obvious, but having many people do a small amount beats a few people doing a lot every time! It might require extra coordination upfront, but in the end it's worth it — you've created a more sustainable organization and your crew will have less burnout and frustration.

- **Communicate, communicate, communicate** — volunteers want to know why they are doing a specific job, how it's going (money raised, amount of people helped, etc.), and they want to know the results of their work. Take the time to develop deeper personal/emotional connections and develop relationships. And don't forget the clear message you developed in Strategy #1, and repeat it often!

- **Ask for ideas** — you'll be surprised every time you ask your volunteers for ideas. They might not know the big picture in the same way that staff does, but they often have new/better/exciting ideas. If you involve your volunteers early in the strategy development process, you'll get enthusiastic, invested supporters. And don't forget to debrief afterward to discuss what went well and lessons learned for next time.

- **Goal-setting** — involve your volunteers in the overall goal-setting process, and also ask them to set individual goals and intentions. Always follow up and communicate about goal completion. It keeps them focused and shows you care about them in addition to the mission.

- **People development** — your volunteers have a natural need to keep progressing and moving forward. By using all the ideas in this section, you can bring them along on a journey where they are always growing into new and more significant levels of contribution and responsibility — and you are continually creating future leaders in the organization.

- **Have volunteer projects ready** — many of the best organizations have a "volunteer projects archive" so when volunteers show up, they can utilize the talent on the spot to do meaningful work. The best way to lose volunteers is to say, "Gee, I'm not sure how you can help. Let me see…"

Tip: Have a file of at-the-ready projects, big and small. Down Home Ranch in Austin (www.DownHomeRanch.org) attracts many local businesses and university teams because they are always prepared for the arrival of individual and group volunteers.

3 key takeaways:

1. Find what your volunteers really want, then give it to them

2. Brainstorm all possible donor objections with your team and develop great messages

3. Take action today by asking volunteers to step forward, by using targeted communications, by asking for referrals, and by appealing to people with the special skills you need

"People don't know what they want until you show it to them." ~Steve Jobs

Chapter 3: the third Power Strategy — who you need to know to raise more money

The third Power Success Strategy is about targeting. It's yet another way of saying "focusing", and we've already introduced a number of concepts in relation to finding the volunteers that are your nonprofit's engine — now let's find donors.

We're all great at qualitative assessments (*"They love us! They come to all our events!"*), but it's time to get quantitative and take a truly objective look at these critical relationships.

Identify potential donors

We've covered quite a bit of the identification process in the second Power Success Strategy. Finding donors is a lot like finding volunteers, and we'll re-visit some key concepts and focus them on donors here.

Low-hanging fruit, part 2: now monetize it!

These are the people you are confident will give. Maybe they've given in the past or maybe they have benefited directly and successfully from your organization's mission. If your nonprofit is succeeding in its mission, you'll be developing new low-hanging fruit regularly. Don't overlook these willing donors as you take time to develop a wider strategy — start here! But just like volunteers, don't ask the same folks over and over — or you'll see them drop away.

Remember not to expend huge amounts of effort here. If you have misjudged a potential donor, just move them to the "later" list and work the rest of the tools we describe in this chapter — it's the 80/20 Rule.

Likely sympathizers, part 2: now monetize it!

Identifying and listing likely sympathizers will help you create the appropriate pool of potential donors to focus on NOW. In this chapter, we'll take you through a process to group these people and identify where to put your short-term and long-term energies.

How can you quickly add to this list if it isn't very big? Referrals. Just ask your people. Again, re-visit the volunteer targeting steps and apply them to donors.

Beware the myth of the corporate solution

A hot current topic in the fundraising world is corporate matching funds and challenge grants. They are a very useful tactic, but they're not a magic bullet! No matter what tactic you are pursuing, it all begins and ends with individual relationships rather than relying on large corporations to wave a magic wand.

Classify donors through the "6 Ps"

This is the most important exercise you will ever do to identify and nurture individual donors. We don't say that lightly, and it's based on our experience working with nonprofits that think they have this one nailed, only to discover that a big business approach identifies glaring gaps between their reality and long-held opinions. Really. Do this one.

It's time to get very honest about where you stand with each donor or potential donor. If you are looking to expand your donor group (and we know you are!), consider developing a prototype donor based on the criteria described below — knowing your current and future targets will help you use that 80/20 Rule to your advantage, and you can expend 20% of the effort to identify 80% of the donations. Honesty and clarity are key here, because idealizing donors can lead to disappointment, and worse, wasted time and resources.

> *This is the most important exercise you will ever do to identify and nurture individual donors.*

1. Platform

Why is the donor interested in this cause? Understanding motivations are critical to developing a plan of action around this (potential) donor, so you should be quite clear on why they might be interested in supporting your organization at a higher level.

People are complex, and there could be one or many reasons. For this purpose, identify the #1 top reason and consider any other strong reasons they might be involved.

Do they have a PERSONAL platform, agenda, or issue?

- They know or love someone who is affected by your cause

- Someone they know is involved and they would like to hang out with them or please them

- They see there is a potential to really make a difference

- Donating is aligned with their family or cultural values

Do they have a BUSINESS platform, agenda, or issue? Some examples of this might be:

- Demonstrating community involvement for a resume or new job/promotion opportunity

- Networking with other people that could advance their careers or businesses

- Gaining leadership experience (by chairing a fundraiser, perhaps)

Whatever their platform might be, understanding it will give you a huge edge in meeting their need and being the recipient of their generosity.

> **TIP:** Avoid the temptation to think they care just because they want to help a good cause. Why YOUR cause?

2. Passion

How strong is their current level of interest in this cause? Are they a casual fan, or are they deeply committed? Be very objective here — in our experience, this is the single area where most people overestimate the level of interest of their targets, and end up underestimating the real work needed to close their financial gaps.

In assessing the level of support your (potential) donor has for your nonprofit, assign an overall value from the following options — when in doubt, chose the lower value:

+50   **Passionate** — deeply committed and gives regularly and significantly

+40   **Enthusiastic** — supports you with their time and donations

+30   **Supporting** — has donated multiple times and is likely to show up at events

+20   **Accepting** — occasional donor likely to say nice things about your organization

+10   **Open** — supports your cause and is likely to donate if you make a good case

0   **Neutral**

-10   **Indifferent** — hasn't thought about your mission and may support other nonprofits

-20   **Skeptical** — doesn't understand your mission and isn't very interested in it

-30   **Avoiding** — has other concerns that they consider more important

-40   **Challenging** — openly critical of your organization and/or your mission

-50   **Opposing** — actively works against your organization's goals

This isn't an evaluation of what they've already given or even committed to — it's an indicator of their level of supportiveness for your organization (which is an indicator of FUTURE support).

This is a great group exercise, where you can ask probing questions:

- What makes you think this person has earned the preference rating assigned?

- Do other members of the team agree with the assessment?

- Have you considered other factors that might affect your assessment? (Time of year, a student graduating from a school that is supported, health issues, etc.?)

- How "sticky" is their passion — what would it take to pull their support? A lot or a little?

Assessments are likely to change over time, so make this an annual exercise — it is worth the time! There are dollar$ attached to it.

3. Potential

How much can a donor potentially give? It's a tricky question, but it's a critical component of your planning process — the resources it takes to woo a major donor would not be best spent on a donor who simply does not have the resources.

Using a point scale, rate the giving power of the potential donor:

Highest giving power rating: +5 = $ _____
Lowest giving power rating: -5 = $ _____

What makes you think this person has earned the giving power rating assigned? Do other members of the team agree with the giving power assessment?

> **TIP:** You may want to assign a $ range from +5 to -5 to help you create levels of potential giving.

If your potential donors are passionate but don't have monetary resources, they can be converted into dedicated volunteers that have influence and responsibilities that will honor their passion. Circumstances change, and these types of donors/volunteers can grow into a philanthropic role, and in the meantime they can influence many others to participate and give — it's a win-win.

4. Prospect

How likely is the donor to give to your organization? The good news is that they support the cause that you support, but there may be many other options for their gift. Based on the information they already have, how likely are they to give to YOUR organization, and are they giving you as much as they can? Be very clear, and rank them honestly:

+50   **Raving Fan** — your organization is their main giving focus for this cause

+40   **Regular Giver** — already gives regularly and dependably with commitment

+30   **Supporter** — giving, but may be doing so out of habit

+20   **Accepting** — occasionally gives based on specific appeals

+10   **Open** — has given, but not lately

0   **Neutral**

-10   **Indifferent** — has another organization in mind with a similar mission

-20   **Skeptical** — pretty convinced your organization isn't right for their giving (because of your track record, size, staff, communication quality, etc.)

-30   **Avoiding** — may be very involved with a competing organization

-40   **Challenging** — had a bad experience with your organization in the past

-50   **Opposing** — actively works against your fundraising efforts

5. Position

What is their role in making the decision to write a check? You can convince some people all day long, but they don't necessarily write the checks. Be clear what role each contact has in appealing to each donor in the decision making process:

- **Gatekeeper** — responsible for "weeding out": they can say "no" but not "yes"

- **Linker** — can help link your cause to the political, cultural or strategic issues of the corporate or personal donor

- **Recommender** — responsible for input for recommendation or selection of your organization

- **Approver** — approves the financial or legal aspects after a choice is made

- **Power Sponsor** — has enough power to help you, and a part in the decision making process

- **Decision-Maker** — has the formal and final responsibility for writing a check

Positions can be difficult to assess — what makes you think this person has this position in the decision-making process? Do other members of the team agree? Sometimes you have to ask your contacts hard clarifying questions to better understand Position. Don't be afraid to ask them exactly what position they have!

TIP: Influencers and Decision-Makers are both important to nurture, leading to donor dollar$. Just be sure you know who is which.

Once again, the positions people play in this process are likely to change over time, so be sure to reassess this aspect at least yearly.

6. Plan

The plan includes the tactics you will use to actually raise money efficiently and successfully from the donors you've identified.

Now that you've taken a hard look at current and potential donors (and donor types), how exactly are we going to reach them and guide them to give? Converting prospects into dependable donors is the topic of the next Power Success Strategy, so we are just touching on it here.

The goal? Create raving fans!

Business guru Ken Blanchard coined the term, and it's a great one. Creating raving fans of your organization means exceeding their expectations in everything you do, providing value, accomplishing your mission, over-communicating, and meeting their needs. This chapter talks about identifying those needs — now go meet and exceed them! You can do it if you know where to focus your energies. They'll repay you by becoming passionate, raving fans that help you attract more volunteers and money than you ever dreamed possible.

3 key takeaways:

1. Ignore the low-hanging fruit at your own peril

2. Classify your potential donors by using the 6 Ps

3. Create raving fans!

"Asking for and receiving help is a way to prime the pump of generosity."
~Jay Perry

Chapter 4: the fourth Power Success Strategy — how you can turn your relationships into cash

"We have a great cause, so how come donors don't just come knocking on our door?"

"I know she's got tons of money and gives to other causes — how come she isn't giving to ours?"

"I'm uncomfortable asking people for money."

How invested are your donors? Do you have a personal connection with them? Do you know why they have supported your organization or why they might in the future?

The fourth Power Success Strategy is about building relationships with your donors and converting those relationships into donations. The benefits are great, but this is a step that is often overlooked — until donors start to fade away. In fact, relationships are key to success on all fronts, so it's also about building great relationships with your staff, volunteers and board.

The authors of this book come from the world of sales consulting and marketing. In our world, sometimes there is no tangible "product" that you can buy on a shelf — you may be selling peoples' skills or talents. So marketing is really about building relationships. And building relationships is about building trust and confidence in your people and your organization. Our people deliver great quality, and they also meet and exceed the needs of their clients.

TIP: For nonprofits, scarce resources mean you must deliver superior quality in relationships, communications, and (of course) in serving the clients you were organized to serve — that's the best way to develop relationships that pay off in donations.

In recent years, we have seen a huge shift in the economy — sometimes we forget that such things are somewhat cyclical in nature and downturns will always occur, and everything will eventually improve. The bottom line is that we need to remember to expect the best and plan for the worst. Doing the work on donor planning will pay off. (A note: this isn't a book about overall strategic planning, and we are focusing here on the planning around converting relationships into donors.)

What's in it for me? Part 2

Why should corporations and individual donors care? You must speak to their agendas. Corporations often discuss their agendas publicly through SEC filings, press releases, company websites, newspaper stories, blog postings and listings of projects they already support. Google is your friend to research this type of information. Corporations usually even have a designated person on their staff to answer questions about their giving policies. Call them!

Beyond corporate giving policies, corporate executives also have agendas. A big executive can push their company from within, and individual donors are almost entirely driven by their enthusiasm for a cause — you've used Power Success Strategy #1 to focus your Impact Statement, and now they need to hear it.

The 6 Ps, part 2: now monetize it!

In the last chapter we applied the 6 Ps to the relationships you have with donors and potential donors. In this chapter we'll look at the 6 Ps again and take that information and use it to actually raise money. This is where you develop a full picture of the potential donor and a plan for the best way to appeal to them. Warning: one size does NOT fit all.

Using the 80/20 Rule, you will be able to identify the core group of potential donors who you can approach now — hit your low-hanging fruit early. The important next steps are in analyzing what it will take to get your other high potential donors up the ladder — and this is the time to develop a specific action plan around each one. Using the 6Ps, you can identify these people and brainstorm a plan to reach them — the possibilities are endless and you will be as successful as your level of creativity will allow.

How invested are your donors?
Do you have a personal connection with them?

1. Platform

You have identified what ties your donor to your cause. Your action plan must include a way to validate their platform/agenda. For example, if your potential donor is a fan of a particular art form, make sure they have special invitations and seats to any performances, let them be a part of the backstage committee, have them form (or join) a strategy committee to develop ways to reach other arts lover donors, or ask them to host a dinner party for other arts lovers and have your artists give a performance.

The key is to expose them to the reason that ties them to your organization.

2. Passion

If your potential donor is excited about your cause, then you're way ahead. But if they fall lower on the scale than "Passionate", then they might need a little push — this is where strong communication and a bit of marketing come in. Make the case by touting the impact and transformation created by your organization's mission. Don't just assume they are reading the newsletter — make it personal. For example, develop a class that explains the ins and outs of your cause, have immersion events where the potential donors interact with people who are being helped, ask them to mentor someone from the affected community as a buddy/big brother/big sister — anything to help them build a personal connection and a way to get more involved.

Remember our rating scale:

+50　**Passionate** — deeply committed and gives regularly and significantly

+40　**Enthusiastic** — supports you with their time and donations

+30　**Supporting** — has donated multiple times and is likely to show up at events

+20　**Accepting** — occasional donor likely to say nice things about your organization

+10　**Open** — supports your cause and is likely to donate if you make a good case

　0　**Neutral**

-10　**Indifferent** — hasn't thought about your mission and may support other nonprofits

-20　**Skeptical** — doesn't understand your mission and isn't very interested in it

-30　**Avoiding** — has other concerns that they consider more important

-40　**Challenging** — openly critical of your organization and/or your mission

-50　**Opposing** — actively works against your organization's goals

If your donor is at Neutral or lower, then they are unlikely to be in your top 20% of short-term donors. This isn't a bad thing; it just means they need more information. If they fall extremely low, ask yourself if it is worth the time at all — if the answer is yes, then the plan for that donor must include ways for you to build a case.

And remember, building a personal connection is your ticket to success.

3. Potential

You've identified high potential donors, and it's time to develop your plan to make sure they know how much change they can effect by their donation and how valuable they are to your success. Whether you appeal to the ego, altruism, desire for connection, or just being part of a great club, your plan should be clear and carried out fully — don't drop the ball on this one!

For example, consider having an awards event and honor these high potential donors, offer to ghost-write an article by them in a local paper about your organization, name something after them (from seats in a theater all the way up to a whole building!), or ask them to be the title chair of an event (then you do the work and only ask them to invite their generous friends).

As we discussed in the last chapter, if your potential donors don't have the resources to become major donors, they can be converted into dedicated volunteers that have influence and responsibilities that will honor their passion. These types of volunteers may become donors in the future and can influence many others to participate and give until then.

Remember to treat your high potential donors with the honors they deserve. Let them know how much you appreciate them.

4. Prospect

If you have assessed your donor as a Raving Fan or a Regular Giver, then they qualify as low-hanging fruit. Communicate with them and show them how much their support means. You'll need a plan for potential donors who may be at the Indifferent up to Supporter level — naturally it involves progressively more effort to convince them to give to your organization, but these people are what we call "warm prospects" in big business.

For example, any possible way to communicate your Impact Statement is a good one (newsletters, emails or blogs), and a personal touch can move people up through the scale (referrals, personal invitations from Raving Fans and Regular Givers, or inclusion in special events). Follow the 80/20 Rule and leave the hard work for another time with anyone ranked below Indifferent.

Remember our ranking scale:

+50   **Raving Fan** — your organization is their main giving focus for this cause

+40   **Regular Giver** — already gives regularly and dependably

+30   **Supporter** — giving, but may be doing so out of habit

+20   **Accepting** — occasionally gives based on specific appeals

+10   **Open** — has given, but not lately

  0   **Neutral**

-10   **Indifferent** — has another organization in mind with a similar mission

-20   **Skeptical** — suspects your organization isn't right for their giving (because of your track record, size, staff, communication quality, etc.)

-30   **Avoiding** — may be very involved with a competing organization

-40   **Challenging** — had a bad experience with your organization in the past

-50   **Opposing** — actively works against your fundraising efforts

Communication is your key to success for viable donors on the Prospect scale.

> **TIP:** Create a fantastic sample donor request letter and have your inner circle send it on their letterhead to their extended network — ask your board, Raving Fans and volunteers.

5. Position

If they're a Decision-Maker or a Power Sponsor, your action plan is clearer — they get the most attention! For the other categories, look at your potential donor's overall feelings and assess what specific tactics you want to try. Be clear — if you're dealing with a Gatekeeper, for example, give yourself specific steps and a timeframe on getting through them to a Decision-Maker or Approver. All roles on the list are important, but it is critical to know who really cuts the check and who has other influence — this way you can manage time and expectations well.

For example, Position is usually combined with one or more of the first 4 Ps in coming up with an action plan. If they are a Decision-Maker or a Power Sponsor, the ideas we described for Potential will probably apply, as will any of the other ideas in this chapter, frankly — these are high priority targets for you and should be getting a high degree of attention. The 80/20 Rule will be demonstrated to you very clearly if these people join your team!

Here are the categories again for reference:

- **Gatekeeper** — responsible for "weeding out" on behalf of the Decision-Maker; they can say "no" but not "yes" (only the Decision-Maker gives the final "yes")

- **Linker** — can help link your cause to the political, cultural or strategic issues of the corporate or personal donor

- **Recommender** — responsible for input or recommendation on the selection of your organization; these can be wealth managers or attorneys, for example

- **Approver** — approves the financial or legal aspects after a choice is made; it could be an accountant or a company CFO

- **Power Sponsor** — has a big issue, a preference for the nonprofit, enough power to help you and a part in the decision-making process

- **Decision-Maker** — has the formal responsibility and "owns" the wallet

If you have to pick one of the 6 Ps to concentrate on, this is the one!

6. Plan

So here we are at the plan. It's multi-dimensional, and each one of the previous 5 Ps has its own endless list of possible action items, so be creative!

There are some important questions to keep in mind on planning:

- How do you win their heart, and what are the specific action items it takes to get there?

- If you can't win their dollars, how else might this relationship be useful? Perhaps they can serve as a Linker or Recommender to an ultimate Decision-Maker.

- Through the process, can you identify other people in the organization that may be Decision-Makers?

- What are the objections that might come up in the process, and how have you addressed them? Can you build the answers into the planning process before they come up as objections?

Plan tips

Whichever way you take your plan, here a few things to keep in mind as you develop your own individualized way of reaching your high potential donors, volunteers and even new board members:

- **Communication.** We've talked a lot about this, and we know it starts by creating an Impact Statement and repeating it often. And don't forget that communication goes both ways — ask for input and listen to the answers, then act on it.

- **Connection.** The goal is always about creating a deeper personal/emotional connection. Make sure you are sharing your own personal story and the stories of others, and include site visits and exposure to the people helped by your organization so that stories have a basis in reality.

- **Proof.** Use your performance statistics to make your case and build your credibility. Facts are needed to support the emotional business case. Show progress!

- **Credibility.** Consider pumping up the credibility of your nonprofit and its executives through articles, blogs and podcasts, plus have them speak at events and participate in public service groups. Have your big name Raving Fans speak up for you too.

- **Leverage.** Leverage your donors' networks by asking for referrals and asking donors to send out materials to people who may not be on your mailing list (yet).

- **Long-term.** This is an exception to the 80/20 Rule in some respects, but pay attention to your future donors. A great example is the young professional programs that opera companies and theaters have in place — up and coming executives are offered cheap seats, special networking nights, and cocktail parties to get them in the door and build their loyalty early and over time.

- **Investors.** Never forget that your donors, volunteers and board members are investors in a social cause — your organization is really just a way for them to help meet a community's need. In business, we judge our progress by our profit, but social investors also measure their progress in the positive returns to society. So make sure they see how their investment pays off.

3 key takeaways:

1. You need great relationships to generate great donations

2. Understand your donors and the needs that drive them

3. Have an efficient plan and stick to it

"Greatest waste of time? Trying to 'convert' non-believers. Instead, surround 'em. That is, you don't 'convert.' They 'discover' — come to appreciate what you're doing because a couple of their pals have joined up." ~Tom Peters

Chapter 5: the fifth Power Success Strategy — what thinking bigger does for you

If you think small, small things will happen. If you think big, anything can happen. Which do you choose?

It seems obvious, and you're already probably thinking about how much it will cost, who will do the work, and will anyone really want to support your organization any more than they already do. A lot of people say no to nonprofits — your organization is important to them but they just have other priorities, or money is scarce, or there aren't enough hours in the day, or… the list goes on.

Have you heard the phrase "think globally, act locally?" It has been used in various contexts since the early 1900s, but our society has moved very swiftly into a globalized village due to the Internet. Nonprofits ran the same way for decades — centuries — and suddenly… boom. 25 years ago there wasn't an Internet, there wasn't even email. We thought and acted locally, and thinking beyond that only meant sending out appeals to other states via direct mail or newsletters. It was a simpler time, but somebody out there thought that communications could be global. And so here we are.

It isn't just about communications and the Internet. Sometimes it's about thinking outside our niche. Here's an example from an organization that Mari-Anne works with:

When Golden Heart Ranch (GHR) was conceiving a conference on living communities for disabled adults, they thought of bringing in people who already ran farms and ranches in California. Mari-Anne suggested expanding it beyond a local focus to include the broader needs of special needs adults across North America as a way to expand the eminence of GHR. The FRED Conference was a tremendous success, and the result was that almost every state and Canada was represented that first year. A huge bonus result was that FRED helped connect investors interested in supporting the purchase of land to those seeking to build new communities! Not only did FRED help put GHR on the national map, this yearly event has gone on to create a powerful coalition of like-minded organizations to expand housing and employment for adults with special needs. (See www. fredconference.org for more information).

Love the messenger

How are you delivering YOUR message? Direct mail? Emails? Do you have a website that is being used strategically and regularly? Social media — Facebook, Twitter, etc.? We can hear you right now:

"those things aren't really performing as well as we'd hoped."

"we don't have the money for a full-time web person."

"nobody reads their mail anymore."

"we end up in a lot of spam folders."

The world is changing much faster than any of us could have ever anticipated. But a new world of connectivity is here, and with it comes a lot of opportunity to leap into a faster and better way of getting your message out globally, while serving the community your organization targets.

The reason social media hasn't clicked for all nonprofits is that this is still about relationships. For nonprofits, social media is a tactic to build relationships; it isn't a relationship by itself.

Social media doesn't need to be a mystery. It's changing every day, and it must be tailored to the needs, resources and strategic plans for each organization. A comprehensive look at social media is the topic of another book, but the key here is to think of how it can serve you in creating relationships.

For nonprofits, social media is a tactic to build relationships; it isn't a relationship by itself.

Is direct mail dead?

No, but it's on life support. Just like social media, it has a specific role to play in helping you create relationships and find a pool of donors and volunteers. It's expensive in relative terms, and Facebook ads and other micro-targeted Internet communications may be a smarter use for your dollars. But holding a special invitation in your hands can be much more effective than getting an email, so nonprofits must be thoughtful and very selective in how they use direct mail.

Collaboration: expand your thinking beyond "competition"

We believe in abundance. Abundance means there is more than enough for everyone, and any energy we waste on worrying about being "beaten" by the competition is just that — a waste. Try re-tooling your definition and embrace the abundance that comes from collaboration. But, DO know what others are doing and how you fit into the bigger picture, then look for ways to partner with them. You just might extend your resources exponentially!

Competitive research

Thinking big means looking at the landscape of what other organizations are doing. In business, we call these "best practices", and it is in your best interest to stay on top of trends and successes across the nonprofit spectrum. Make a list and have a brainstorming session — how can these great ideas be used or adapted for your success? (Remember, you aren't stealing ideas — it's "leveraging").

Alliances

It is tempting to think of other nonprofits as competitors — especially ones that serve your same cause. Don't fall into that trap. Start to consider how you can think collaboratively. In the marketing world, we love to align with other organizations and promote each other's events, courses, conferences and products — we get access to a whole new email list, which means we are reaching many more people. These people generally won't pick "either or", they just might pick you both! Think about it. And consider how you might divide and conquer for the greater mission.

A thinking big example

After a successful conference, the leader created a Facebook group and asked the participants to put up a tip for next year's attendees. They did, but many also took the time to rave about how great the event had been. The leader then did a screen capture of the comments page and put it in a marketing email. The lesson: Last year's attendees are an ASSET that can be used to market next year's event.

What assets does your organization have and how can you use them?

3 key takeaways:

1. Think globally, act locally

2. Embrace the future of communications

3. Collaborate with the competition — and "leverage" ideas

"If you think big, then it's going to be big." ~Emeril Lagasse

Chapter 6: tips on how you can do all this and keep your sanity

Whew. You might be thinking you have enough to do already. If you're getting acceptable results from your operations and fundraising, then you're probably doing just fine. The 80/20 Rule doesn't apply here, though — we'd wager there are less than 1% of nonprofits that are doing such a complete job that they can't use these 5 Power Success Strategies to show real operational and financial improvement.

The bottom line is that doing the RIGHT things will move you forward. It's still all about focus. You won't be working harder, you'll be working smarter and more efficiently, and that feeling of "spinning your wheels" and making dubious progress will ease up. Peace of mind is a good thing!

It takes courage and it takes discipline.
You've got both.

So break it down, follow the 5 Power Success Strategies, and watch yourself soar. Here are a few tips to keep your hands firmly on the wheel:

Set intentions

Goals, vision, plans — it's all in the same basket. We believe in setting SMART goals:

- **Specific** — we will choose exact numbers

- **Measurable** — our goals will include specific numbers, amounts, dates

- **Attainable** — the goal can actually be achieved

- **Relevant** — our results will move our cause forward

- **Timely** — we will achieve the goal on a specific date

Plans help you keep to the 80/20 Rule — the minute you start expending more than 20% of the effort to get less than 80% of the possible results is the minute you need to take a deep breath and move away from the perfectionism track. Stop and re-group and plan. You can do it!

Let it go

We've talked about the 80/20 Rule a lot. It's a great tool, and can serve as your criteria for letting go of projects that aren't producing results. You can always put things off that don't fit into the top 20% of effort/80% of results — but we doubt you'll get back to unproductive effort anytime soon. It takes courage and it takes discipline. You've got both.

Don't invent (m)any wheels

Creating something from scratch is hard work. Do you have the time? The answer is to be aware of what has worked for you, and to study your competitors and other nonprofits. Earlier we suggested that you steal from the best and adapt it to your own needs — don't just steal from big business; use whatever works, with integrity. Serve your cause and stop worrying so much about originality — you'll put your own spin on it anyway.

Share your voice

We want to hear from you. How did you use the 5 Power Success Strategies to jump to the next level, save time, attract more volunteers, and generate more donations? Leave us a comment at the Profit in Nonprofit page on Facebook, and send us your story at Info@ProfitInNonprofit.com or shoot us an email and let us interview you — you may be a part of our next book!

Go for it!

You have unlimited power — use it efficiently and keep your nonprofit on the road to success.

What's next for us at Nonprofit Success Strategies?

Be sure to like the Profit in Nonprofit page on Facebook and opt in to the email list on our site at www.ProfitinNonprofit.com. We have some great information coming out soon, and we're planning future workshops — you'll be the first to know! We'll never sell or rent your contact information to ANYONE, so sign up today!

About the authors

The authors of this book have a combined total of over 50 years of experience as marketing leaders at multi-billion dollar companies and have served on numerous nonprofit boards. Just like most volunteers, we were drawn to found or serve nonprofits based on our own interests: Mari-Anne Kehler is inspired by her son, a happy young adult named Liam who happens to be autistic. Former operatic tenor Andrew Bird has spent his life supporting the arts and mentorship programs.

Mari-Anne Kehler

Mari-Anne is an advisory board member of Golden Heart Ranch, and on its behalf launched the FRED Conference in 2012 as Director. FRED is the preeminent international conference bringing parents and professionals together to advance opportunities for adults with special needs to find homes and employment and live with purpose.

Mari-Anne has been active in the community in the areas of disability awareness and fundraising and in mentoring families and professionals for almost two decades. Her particular specialty is creating successful transition strategies to optimize the special needs journey into adulthood.

Serving on numerous nonprofit boards supporting children, education and the special needs community such as Project Miracle and the Center for Learning Unlimited, she was past President of the Los Angeles board of Autism Speaks, the primary global organization focused on research and advocacy for autism.

Mari-Anne has held sales, marketing and business development leadership roles at top organizations for almost three decades. She served as a national marketing leader for Deloitte Services LP where she held a number of positions on the Marketing and Business Development leadership team, including heading up National Tax marketing and marketing/business development of the Pacific Southwest region. She has also been a highly rated trainer of senior level talent at the globally renowned Deloitte University.

Prior to joining Deloitte she led West Coast regional marketing efforts for a division of Nestle. She began her career on Wall Street at Morgan Stanley, and has also held director positions at Bertelsmann Entertainment and Grey Direct, overall gaining insights in various industries including finance, entertainment, media and consumer products.

Mari-Anne studied in the master's program at the University of Santa Monica, with an emphasis in leadership and coaching. She attended the College of Mt. St. Vincent in Riverdale, N.Y., where she received a degree in both English Literature and Business Administration.

Mari-Anne and her husband, Eddie, are proud of their adult son, Liam, who continues to defy limits and professional assessments in his ability to show up as a truly remarkable and productive citizen of the planet. Their family has been impacted by the challenges of raising a special needs child into adulthood and have lived the intensive struggles many families must battle.

She has been a featured speaker at schools, colleges and conferences on the topic of disabilities: awareness, transition to adulthood and the impact on families. With extensive experience in business, she has also coached a number of organizations with her skills in strategy, marketing and board development workshops. She can be reached at Mari-Anne@ProfitinNonprofit.com.

Andrew Bird

A former Deloitte & Touche marketing executive, Andrew Bird ultimately served as Leader of Strategic Marketing Initiatives in the U.S. for the firm. He has over 20 years of experience in nonprofit operations, content marketing, complex project management, marketing strategy, leading diverse teams and developing future leaders.

A true believer in giving back, over the years Andrew has founded two nonprofits, served as executive director of three, and has been a board member of five. He currently serves on the board of Global Brigades, a $15 million+ nonprofit that sends thousands of student volunteers on overseas volunteer missions yearly, and also is deeply involved in expanding the reach of Global Brigades' successful fundraising technology platform, www.Empowered. org. A long-time supporter of mentorship programs, he founded a regional mentoring group at Deloitte and was co-founder of the firm's highly successful and ongoing National Senior Manager Advisory Council group.

Andrew is recognized as an authority on proposal and grant strategy and implementation. His achievements include winning the Marketing Achievement Award from the Association of Accounting Marketing, serving as a keynote speaker on proposal writing for such organizations as the Independent Writers of Chicago, and publishing a series of articles on proposal/grant strategy and implementation for *Svoboda's Business Magazine*. He won the Deloitte Award for Distinction and Excellence from the National Consumer Business Practice and has written proposals worth over $1 billion in new business. He is currently a content marketing consultant to nonprofits and global businesses.

He earned his BS in Business Administration from New York University, an MBA in Finance from Loyola University, and an MA in Spiritual Psychology from the University of Santa Monica (USM), where he continues to volunteer regularly. For USM, he was also a founding team member of SpiritWalk, a fundraiser that has earned over $500,000 for students facing financial challenges since 2010. This event is ongoing, and continues to be executed each year by graduating students. Andrew can be reached at Andrew@ProfitinNonprofit.com.

Acknowledgements

This book is born out of our personal passions for giving back, and our professional experiences in "big business". There are many, many folks who have contributed to the writing of this book, including those who were role models in how to live a purpose-driven life.

At Deloitte, the leaders we tried to emulate were David Thompson, Sharon Allen, Tony Buzzelli and Evan Hochberg. They taught us by their word and led by example, modeling how to effectively "give back" to the community. Dave Porges continues to demonstrate, through ongoing friendship, coaching and his personal commitment, what it means to marry smart business and meaningful service.

Diana O'Brien is a friend, former Deloitte colleague and mentor, and she epitomizes how best to use business Power Strategies to create and lead a successful nonprofit. IMPACT Autism was originally just her vision, and is now helping to change lives for many individuals with autism and related disabilities.

There are too many other nonprofit role models to mention them all, but those in particular who share our passion for leveraging business Power Strategies are our heroes: Steve and Vanessa Atamian (Global Brigades), Elaine Hall (Project Miracle), Laura Shumaker (Camphill Communities CA and Special Hope Foundation), Dr. Rebecca Foo (Switzer Learning Center), Rose Hein (Golden Heart Ranch), Mark Olson (LTO Ventures), Tom and Claudia Storm-Grzywacz (Center for Learning Unlimited), Mark Woodsmall (Spero Vineyard and Autism Speaks), Chantal

Sicile-Kira (Autism College), Drs. Ron and Mary Hulnick and the founding SpiritWalk team (University of Santa Monica), and Dr. Zoe Mailloux — and we thank you.

Before we were in the business world there were two people who by their professions and how they treated others demonstrated the essence of giving back, and that's our moms, Jackie and Peggy. Without their ongoing encouragement, we'd never have landed here. Thanks, Moms! And of course, Eddie and Liam make Mari-Anne's world spin, making everything worth doing.

www.ingramcontent.com/pod-product-compliance
Lightning Source LLC
Chambersburg PA
CBHW071303170526
45165CB00003B/1398

* 9 7 8 1 5 0 0 6 9 9 6 1 1 *